Animal Superpowers
SUPER SPEED

Joanne Mattern

RED
CHAIR
·PRESS·

Animal Superpowers is produced and published by Red Chair Press:

Red Chair Press LLC   PO Box 333   South Egremont, MA 01258-0333

www.redchairpress.com

Publisher's Cataloging-In-Publication Data
Names: Mattern, Joanne, 1963-

Title: Super speed / Joanne Mattern.

Other Titles: Core content library.

Description: South Egremont, MA : Red Chair Press, [2019] | Series: Earth's amazing animals : animal superpowers | Includes glossary, Power Word science term etymology, fact and trivia sidebars. | Includes bibliographical references and index. | Summary: "Flying, swimming, or hopping. Running for cover or running down prey. Some animals on Earth use super speed to survive."--Provided by publisher.

Identifiers: LCCN 2018937240 | ISBN 9781634404242 (library hardcover) | ISBN 9781634404303 (ebook)

Subjects: LCSH: Animal locomotion--Juvenile literature. | Speed--Juvenile literature. | CYAC: Animal locomotion. | Speed.

Classification: LCC QP301 .M38 2019 (print) | LCC QP301 (ebook) | DDC 573.7/9--dc23

Illustrations by Tim Haggerty

Maps by Joe LeMonnier

Photo credits: iStock except Alamy pg. 5, 12, 14, 15, 17, 22, 28

Printed in United States of America

102018 1P CGBS19

Table of Contents

Introduction

Superheroes in books and movies are amazingly fast. They can fly, run, and swim much faster than ordinary humans. Some animals are super-fast too. There are many animal super speeders who could give superheroes in the comics a run for their money!

Super speed helps animals in many ways. If an animal is on the hunt, running or flying super-fast can help it catch its **prey**. Prey animals need super speed as well. Running quickly can help these animals get away from **predators** who want to eat them.

Now, hold onto your hats and get ready to run, fly, and swim with the fastest animals on Earth!

Fast Cat:
The Cheetah

If you saw a cheetah lying in the grass, you wouldn't think it could run that fast. This cat looks lazy as it soaks up the sun. However, looks can fool you. The cheetah is the fastest land animal. These speedy cats can run up to 75 miles (120 km) an hour! And they can go from 0 to 60 in just three seconds.

A cheetah's body is built for running. Its legs are very long. Long legs let the cheetah cover up to 25 feet (7.6 m) in one stride. **Flexible** hips and spine also help the cheetah move quickly. The cat's long tail helps it balance. Its body is light and thin. And its lungs are huge to hold a lot of air while it runs.

Now You Know!

Almost all wild cheetahs live in the African grasslands.

Now You Know!

Unlike most cats, a cheetah's claws are always out. This helps it grip the ground—and grab its prey.

Cheetahs can run fast, but only over short distances. When it sees its prey, the cheetah creeps slowly through the long grass. It gets closer and closer. Finally, it jumps up and **sprints** after its prey. If it can't catch its prey in a few seconds, the cheetah gives up. It can't keep up its speed for long.

Cheetahs usually hunt deer and antelope. However, cheetahs will also eat rabbits and birds. When it is not hunting, the cheetah likes to sleep in the long grass.

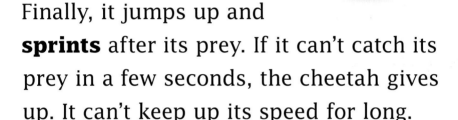

Super Diver:
The Peregrine Falcon

It's a bird! It's a plane! It's Superman! No, *it is a bird*. That zooming, diving creature is a peregrine falcon, the fastest bird in the air.

Peregrine falcons are birds of prey. They eat other birds. Almost any bird can be a meal for a peregrine falcon. Falcons also eat bats.

Peregrine falcons fly high above the ground, looking for their prey. When this bird sees something good to eat, it dives down to grab it. That's when the falcon picks up speed. A falcon can dive up to 240 miles (385 km) an hour.

Power Word: The name *peregrine* comes from the Middle Ages French and Latin words for wandering or traveling around.

Now You Know!

People have trained falcons for hunting for thousands of years.

When a peregrine falcon catches up to its prey, it grabs it with its sharp **talons**. Then it carries its meal to a tree to eat it. These birds also nest in tall buildings. Some even live on bridges or city skyscrapers.

At one time, peregrine falcons were **endangered**. Many were killed by **pesticides**. Today, these speedy birds are back. These falcons live in the cold Arctic tundra of Greenland, Canada, and Russia and in the hot deserts of Chile and north Africa. They live on every continent except Antarctica.

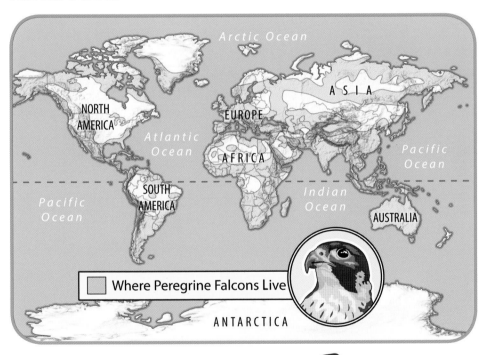

Where Peregrine Falcons Live

Now You Know!

Golden eagles are fast birds too. They can reach speeds of 75-200 miles (120-320 km) per hour when hunting.

Now You Know!

Sailfish are part of a group of fish called billfish. They have a long, sharp bill, or nose.

Ocean Predator:
The Sailfish

Many fish swim fast. But none swims as fast as the sailfish. This fish's body is built for speed!

The sailfish gets its name from the large fin on its back. This fin looks like the sail on a boat. The sail helps the fish swim quickly in the water. Sometimes the sailfish leaps out of the water. When this happens, the fin catches the wind just like the sail on a boat does. Scientists believe that sailfish can zoom along at speeds up to 70 miles (113 km) per hour.

Sailfish live in the warm waters of the Atlantic and Pacific Oceans. They hunt in groups of two or more. Sailfish usually swim into a school of smaller fish and splash around to scatter the smaller fish. Then each sailfish slashes at its prey with its sharp bill. Sailfish also use their sails to make a fence around their prey so none of the smaller fish can escape. *Now that's sneaky!*

A sailfish is usually about six feet (1.8 m) long. However, one was measured at more than ten feet (3 m) long. It weighed more than 140 pounds (63 kg).

Now You Know!

Sailfish eggs hatch just 36 hours after they are laid.

Sailfish hunting sardines

A Speedy Getaway:
The Pronghorn Antelope

Predators are not the only speedy animals in the world. Their prey has to be fast as well. Otherwise, prey animals would have no chance to get away. One of the best examples of an animal that uses speed to escape is the pronghorn antelope.

The pronghorn antelope gets its name from its horns. They bend in different directions. These mammals live only in North America. They prefer grasslands from Texas up to Montana and Saskatchewan in Canada. Animals like coyotes, bobcats, and mountain lions hunt antelope. The antelope **adapted** by developing its own super speed.

Pronghorn Antelope can run long distances.

Now You Know!

Pronghorn antelopes are fast runners, but they are very bad at jumping. They usually go under a fence instead of jumping over it.

Pronghorns are big animals, but they are very light. They are about 4.5 feet (1.4 m) long but weigh only 110 pounds (50 kg). The antelope has light bones and hollow hair. It also has a very large heart and lungs. These features allow the animal to run fast over long distances. The pronghorn antelope can run more than 60 miles (96 km) an hour.

An antelope's feet are also made for speed. This animal's feet have two long, pointed toes. These toes help the antelope take the shock when its hooves hit the ground as it runs.

Now You Know!

Pronghorn antelopes shed their horns and grow new ones each year.

Now You Know!

A group of hares is called a drove.

Hopping Away:
The Hare

Sometimes people get hares and rabbits mixed up. The two animals do look alike. However, they are different **species**. Both animals are fast. But the hare's body makes it a speedy superhero!

A hare's back legs are longer than its front legs. Those powerful back legs help the hare cover long distances when it runs. A hare can run up to 45 miles (72 km) an hour. They can also jump up to 12 feet (3.7 m) in one hop. Hares can be found on every continent except Antarctica. The Brown Hare is very common in Great Britain.

Brown Hare

It's a good thing that hares can run so fast. Many animals prey on hares. They are hunted by coyotes, foxes, bobcats, owls, and hawks. Along with running fast, hares also run in a zigzag pattern. This helps them confuse predators. That gives them a better chance to escape.

When they aren't running from danger, hares are quiet animals. They spend most of their time resting or looking for food. Hares are **herbivores**. They eat grass and seeds.

Hares are born with fur and their eyes are open. Baby hares are called leverets.

Black-naped hare with newly born leveret

A Speedy Thief:
The Frigatebird

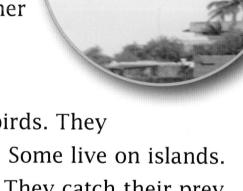

Many animals use speed to catch their prey. But the frigatebird has another trick up its wing. It uses speed to steal!

Frigatebirds are seabirds. They live along the ocean. Some live on islands. These birds eat fish. They catch their prey in the ocean and in large **lagoons**.

Frigatebirds eat fish. They snatch their prey right out of the ocean. But if a frigatebird sees another bird eating a fish, it will zoom over and grab the fish right out of the other animal's claws.

Speedy thieves on watch for food.

Now You Know!

Frigatebirds do not have any enemies in the air. However, rats and other animals eat their eggs out of nests on the ground.

Unlike most birds, frigatebirds lay just one egg at a time.

Now You Know!

Males take care of frigatebird chicks for the first three months. After that, the female takes over.

Frigatebirds are so fast because they have large wings. This bird is only two or three feet (0.6 to 1 m) long, but its wingspan is about 7½ feet (2.3 m). These birds can stay in the air for up to two months! They are high fliers as well. This bird can soar up to 12,000 feet (3.6 km) high.

Although frigatebirds spend most of their lives flying over the ocean, they rarely land on the water. That's because their feathers are not waterproof and they have short legs. So, if they landed on the water, they would sink! It's better to zip along high in the sky.

Speedy Creatures

The animals in this book are among the fastest animals on our planet. It's amazing to think about how fast these animals can run, swim, and fly. Whether they use their speed to hunt or to get away from a hunter, speed is a way for these animals to stay alive.

Superheroes have some amazing powers when it comes to running and flying at super speeds. However, don't forget that animals can be superhero-fast as well.

Glossary

adapted adjusted to new conditions

endangered in danger of dying out

flexible able to bend easily

herbivores animals that eat plants

lagoons areas of salt water separated from the ocean

pesticides poisons used to kill insects and other pests

predator an animal that hunts other animals for food

prey animals that are hunted by other animals for food

species a group of living organisms that are the same

sprints runs fast over a short distance

talons large, strong claws on a bird

More in the Library

Lunis, Natalie. *Peregrine Falcon: Dive, Dive, Dive!* (Blink of an Eye series). Bearport, 2011.

Murray, Julie. *Fastest Animals* (That's Wild! series). Abdo, 2010.

National Geographic Kids: cheetahs https://goo.gl/aLVEJt

Index

About the Author

Joanne Mattern is the author of nearly 350 books for children and teens. She began writing when she was a little girl and just never stopped! Joanne loves nonfiction because she enjoys bringing science topics to life and showing young readers that nonfiction is full of compelling stories! Joanne lives in the Hudson Valley of New York State with her husband, four children, and several pets!